LOSS for LITTLES

A GUIDE FOR CHRISTIAN FAMILIES DEALING WITH DEATH

WRITTEN BY EMILY ANN ADAMS
ILLUSTRATED BY ESTER BALLAM BIGGS

For my Savior, Jesus Christ, who taught me that death is not the end.
And for *all* my angel babies - Daphne, Darcie, Alan, Aiden and Phoebe.
-EAA

For all of the special angels in my life – on both sides of the veil.
-EBB

ISBN: 979-8-9860565-1-7
Library of Congress Control Number: 2022907193
First Edition, May 2022

A Note to Parents

Welcome to Loss for Littles: A Guide for Families Dealing with Death. This book was written from the perspective of my daughter, Daphne, in hopes that other children who have experienced the loss of a loved one, as she did, may be helped along their healing journey.

Sometimes, in the midst of heartbreak, parents or caretakers may not fully prepare their child for exposure to new and unfamiliar terms, rituals, and traditions that revolve around death. Being unprepared for these experiences, on top of navigating feelings of grief, can cause a child to feel vulnerable, confused or afraid.

For most young children, the concepts of death, funerals, and burials are completely foreign until they are confronted with the loss of a loved one. It is important that children have meaningful conversations about these topics with a trusted adult who can guide them through their grief and mentor their healing.

My hope is that this book will allow families a moment of stillness in order to sit down and have essential discussions about loss. This book is a tool meant to assess what the child understands about death, what questions they may have, and how to give them the necessary support for their grief. With that knowledge, please take each section at your own pace and leave plenty of room for connecting and communicating.

As you read through the text, you will come across death-related terms that have been bolded and italicized. I have included a glossary in the back of the book for a full definition on each term, however, it may be valuable to make sure your child understands these words and concepts as you come across them.

Although children may be little, their emotions are big and deserve to be acknowledged and respected. May God guide you and the littles in your care with the assurance that He is with you and that through the power of Jesus Christ's atonement and resurrection, families truly can be together forever.

Hi, my name is Daphne! When I get to know a new friend, like you, I tell them facts about myself. I say that I am ten years old and I love science, reading, and drawing. Next, I might tell them about some of the fun things I do like going to school, taking piano lessons, or playing soccer. A new friend might also ask me about my family, but that's where things get tricky for me to explain.

You see, I have two sisters and two brothers, but only one of my brothers is here on earth with me. When I was five years old, my mom was pregnant with identical twin boys. My little sister Darcie and I were so excited to meet them! But only our brother Alan survived. Our other brother, Aiden, died inside my mom's tummy before he was born.

After Aiden died, I was so sad that he wouldn't be able to live with our family on earth anymore. But I was also comforted knowing that we are an eternal family which means we can all be together again someday.

Maybe you have someone you love who has died and is in heaven too. Perhaps you have recently suffered the death of a sibling, a parent, a grandparent or another loved one, and you have felt how hard it can be to lose someone.

I want to share with you some of the things my family and I have learned about life and death, **grief** and healing in this book. I hope it will help you understand what has happened to the person you love and how you can still feel close to them even when they are gone.

Before we came to earth, we lived in heaven with all the spirit children of God. Heavenly Father presented a plan for us to receive a body through birth to help us grow both physically and spiritually. For us to live on Earth, our spirits were put inside of a body grown inside of our mothers. If you look at your skin, you won't be able to see your spirit, but you can feel it inside through your mind and emotions.

SPIRIT   BODY   BIRTH

EARTH LIFE   DEATH

SPIRIT

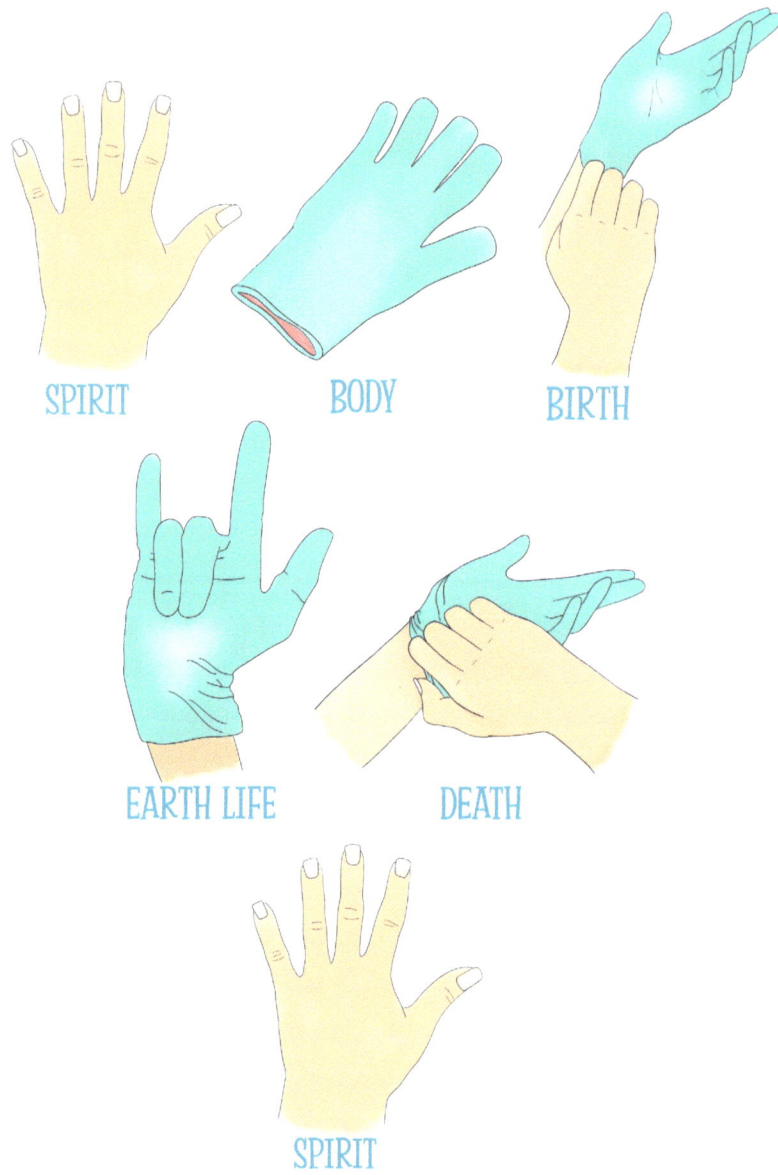

My Dad once explained it like this. He held up his hand and a glove. The glove was flat and floppy and couldn't move on its own, but his hand could wiggle and twist. Dad said our spirit is like our hand and our body is like the glove. When the hand is put inside the glove, like our spirit being put into our body, suddenly the glove can move. But when we take the glove off, it becomes motionless again. This is a good example of what happens when we die and our spirit leaves our body.

Death is when the body and the spirit are separated from one another. That means our body can no longer breathe, see, move, feel or think. However, our spirit lives on and goes back to heaven to be with our Heavenly Father.

Sometimes people don't like to talk about death and dying, so they will use other words to describe what happened. When your loved one died, maybe you heard people say they had "passed away", "moved on", "gone to the other side", or that they were "with Jesus."

When my brother died, someone said we had "lost" the baby. This confused me. If he was lost, I wondered, why hadn't we gone out looking for him? I felt afraid that maybe I would become lost too and that no one would come looking for me.

For a while after Aiden died, I had nightmares about being lost. Over time, I learned that Aiden wasn't actually lost. People just meant he was no longer alive on earth and that his death could not be undone.

The only person who has reversed death was Jesus Christ. When Jesus died, his body and spirit were separated for a time. Through the power of God, Jesus was able to put them back together again. This is called being **resurrected**.

When Jesus comes again a second time, he will help all of God's children who have lived on the earth be reunited with their bodies and spirits forever. After we are resurrected, we will never die again.

Because we do not know when Jesus will come again, for now, death is part of our life on earth. Everyone must be born and everyone must die. There are many different reasons why people die.

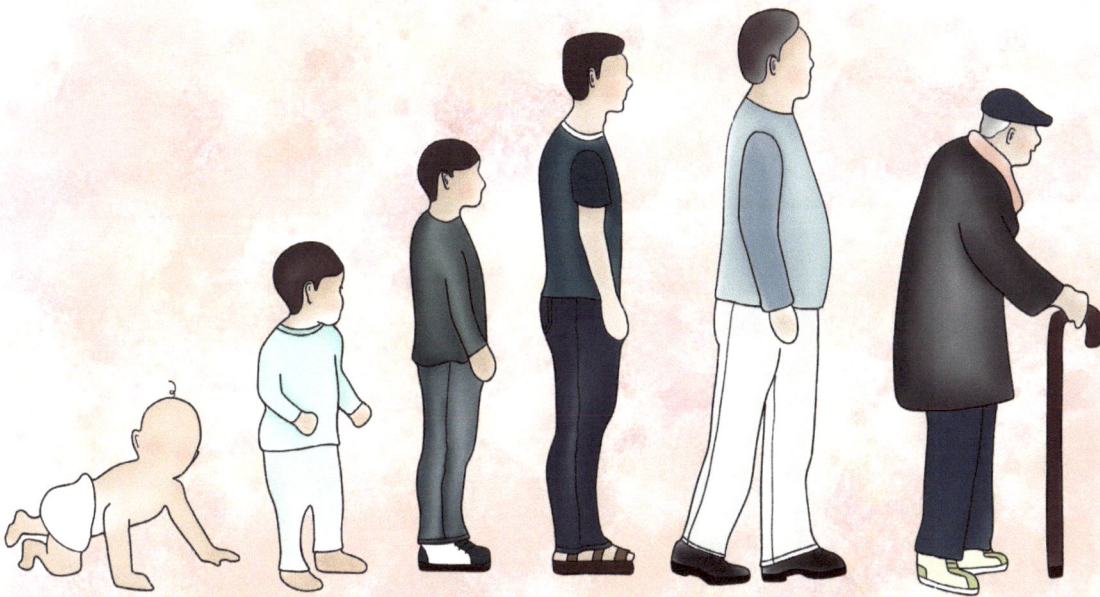

If all goes well, we are born as healthy babies, who grow into children, and then age into adults who live long lives. As we grow old, our bodies begin to wear out until they eventually stop working.

However, some children never get the chance to grow up. Sometimes, when a woman becomes pregnant, the baby may experience problems and die before they are born. When a baby dies in their mother's tummy, this is called a miscarriage or a stillbirth. My brother Aiden was considered stillborn because he never took a breath of air when he was born.

Although it would be wonderful for all of us to live a long, healthy life, sometimes Heavenly Father has a different plan and may bring a person's spirit home to Heaven, through death, before we are ready to be apart from them.

When a person dies, their spirit returns to God and their body is left empty. Depending on the customs of the country you live in, many things may happen to the person's body after they die. In my culture, a family usually has two choices. They can either bury the body in a **casket** (also called a coffin) or they can have the body **cremated** (burned) and keep the ashes in a special container called an **urn**.

After a person has died, special workers called **morticians** or **funeral directors** take the body to a building called a **mortuary** to prepare it to be buried or cremated. While the morticians work, the family decides whether they would like to have a **viewing**, **funeral**, **memorial** or **graveside**. These services are opportunities for the people who knew and loved the person who has died to come together to honor their life.

A viewing is a gathering at a church or **funeral home** where you can see the body of the person who has died one last time. The body has been prepared by the mortician to look peaceful and beautiful and is then laid in their casket, sometimes wearing special religious clothing.

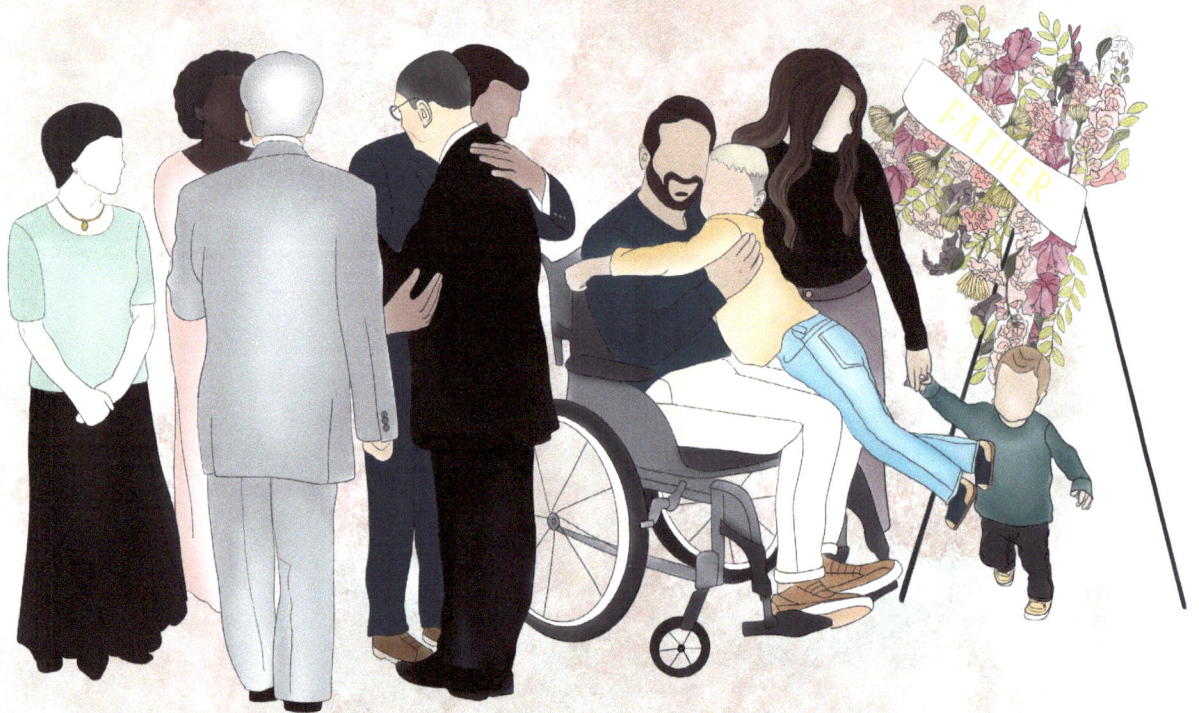

The closest members of the family stand in a line next to the casket to greet the people who have come. When I was at my Great-Grandma's viewing, I noticed the people who came through the line shook hands, hugged, told stories, and often cried or laughed together.

After the viewing, family members and friends come together for a ceremony called a funeral. The funeral service is a program full of songs and talks. Usually, the first speaker will give a **eulogy** which is a short summary of the important events of a person's life. Other speakers may share stories from the person's life, words of comfort, or religious thoughts.

There may be many people crying at the funeral because they will miss the person who has died. You may feel like crying and that's ok. You may also not feel like crying and that's okay too. Everyone experiences loss differently.

Sometimes, people may share memories about your loved one's life that will make you smile or even laugh and that's also okay. Mostly, the viewing and funeral are a time where feelings of grief and love can be shared as a group. Funerals can be a wonderful time for healing to begin.

Once the funeral has ended, the casket is carried by **pallbearers** out of the chapel. Pallbearers are close family members or friends. At my Great-Grandma's funeral, all of her sons and sons-in-laws helped to carry her casket. But at my brother Aiden's funeral, his body was so small that my Dad was able to carry his little white coffin all by himself.

The pallbearers take the casket outside to a special car called a **hearse** that has a large open space to carry the coffin in the back. Once the casket is in the hearse, everyone gets in their cars and follows the hearse in one big line to the **cemetery**, a special place where bodies are buried. This line of cars is called a **funeral procession**.

Once the procession of cars has reached the cemetery, the people get out of their cars and walk to the **grave**, a hole in the ground where the body will be buried. Rows of chairs are set up next to the grave under a canopy where everyone gathers. When everyone is ready, the pallbearers carry the coffin from the hearse to the grave.

Some families choose not to have a viewing or funeral and instead come straight to the cemetery for a graveside service which is basically a funeral outside. At the graveside, there may be more talks, prayers and songs. A religious leader may lead the group in a special prayer to dedicate the grave.

After the graveside, you may leave the cemetery whenever you and your family feel ready. Once everyone has left, the mortuary workers will use a machine to lower the casket into a cement **vault** in the grave which is then covered with dirt. Over time, grass will be planted on top of the dirt and a **headstone** will be placed to mark the spot where the person is buried.

Each grave is marked by a metal plate or a headstone. These markers come in all shapes and sizes. The name of the person buried underneath is carved into the stone as well as their birth and death dates.

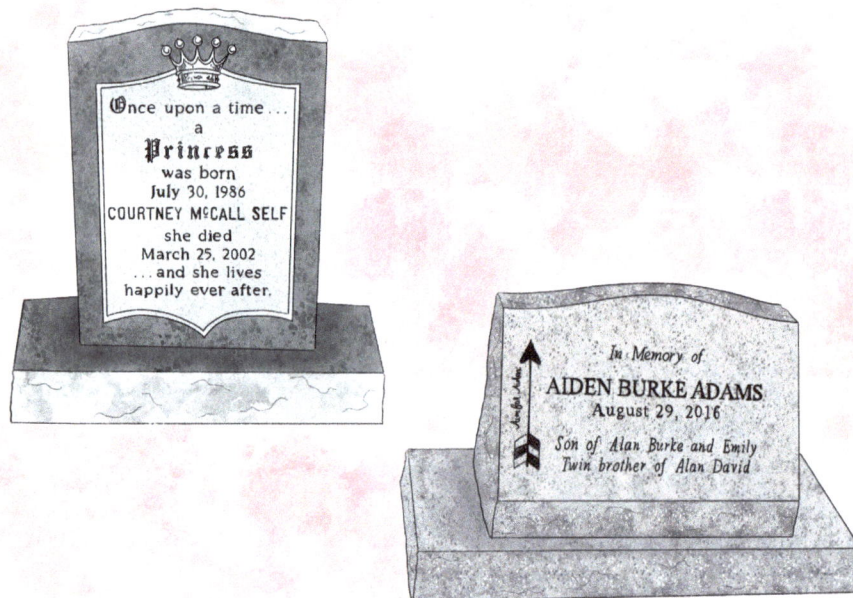

These headstones become special spots that we can return to in the future when we want to remember or honor the person who has died.

After the graveside, relatives and close friends gather together to share a meal. The family may pass a microphone around so people can share their thoughts and memories about the person who has died before everyone says goodbye and goes back home.

After being with so many people all day, you may feel very worn out and in need of some quiet time. It's okay if you want to be alone. It's also okay to want to be with your family to talk with them about what you are feeling and thinking. I remember after my brother's funeral my family was ready to be all by ourselves for a little while.

Over the next few days and weeks, we did some special things to honor Aiden. We planted a white rose bush for him. We put decorations with arrows around the house to remember our new motto to "Aim for Aiden". I drew a picture of me reaching towards heaven and Aiden flying in the sky. We put his things in a memory box so that we could look through it whenever we wanted to feel extra close to him. Do you have any special items that help you remember your loved one?

A few days after the funeral, it seemed as though everyone else went back to their regular life, but our family was different now. I felt like we would never be the way we used to be and, in some ways, I didn't want us to be.

Because we love Aiden, and because you love the person who died in your life, it is normal to feel grief when they are gone.

So, what exactly is grief? Grief is basically heavy sadness that you feel, especially when someone has died. Usually, these feelings of sorrow are the most powerful in the first few days and weeks after a person has died, but grief can last for months, years and even a lifetime!

There is no need to feel ashamed of the times you feel sad as it is just part of missing your loved one. As you begin to heal, you may still feel moments of deep sorrow, but you will be able to feel happier for longer spaces in-between.

Some people feel guilty if they allow themselves to laugh and be happy after someone they love has died. But guess what? Your loved one doesn't want you to be sad all the time. Remember, their spirit lives on! And the spirit of your loved one wants you to be happy again so you can continue to learn and grow. In fact, one of the greatest ways you can show them that you loved them is by becoming a better person because they died. Grief can actually help us grow in many positive ways!

That might sound strange. How could a person dying become something positive? For me, I've noticed that after Aiden's death, I became a better friend to others. I notice when people are sad and I try to find ways to cheer them up. My family and I have gained a deeper testimony that families really can be together forever. We also realize that every day we are alive is a gift from God, so we try our best to make each day a good one.

Choosing to grow and become better people because of grief can be very difficult. The great news is, you don't have to try to do it alone! You have so many people on your side who want to help you succeed. These people include your family, friends, teachers, and church leaders who can talk with you about your sadness.

There are also special doctors called **therapists** or **counselors** for your mind and emotions. They have been trained to talk with children and adults about the hard things they have gone through and help them in their healing journey.

Your community may offer **support groups** you can attend or your family may find a group online of others who have gone through a similar kind of loss. People who reach out to others they can trust and share what they are feeling heal much more quickly than those who keep their emotions hidden and quiet inside.

As nice as it is to have family, friends, teachers, and others helping us in our healing journey, none can compare to having our Savior, Jesus Christ, wrapping His arms around us and carrying us through the trials of our lives. Because of the **atonement** of Jesus Christ, He is the only person who truly understands exactly what we are thinking and feeling and how best to help us. When we turn our hearts to Him and talk with Him through prayer, He can heal us.

Because of Jesus, we have the knowledge that death is not the end. Because of His atonement and resurrection, we can put our trust in Him and believe that we will see our loved ones who have died again.

As I aim to follow in the footsteps of Jesus Christ, I am also aiming for Aiden and any other loved ones who may pass away before I do. I have faith that Aiden's spirit is happy and well with Heavenly Father and Jesus. I know I will see my brother again and you will see your loved one who has passed away too. I can't wait for the day we will all get to be together again - forever!

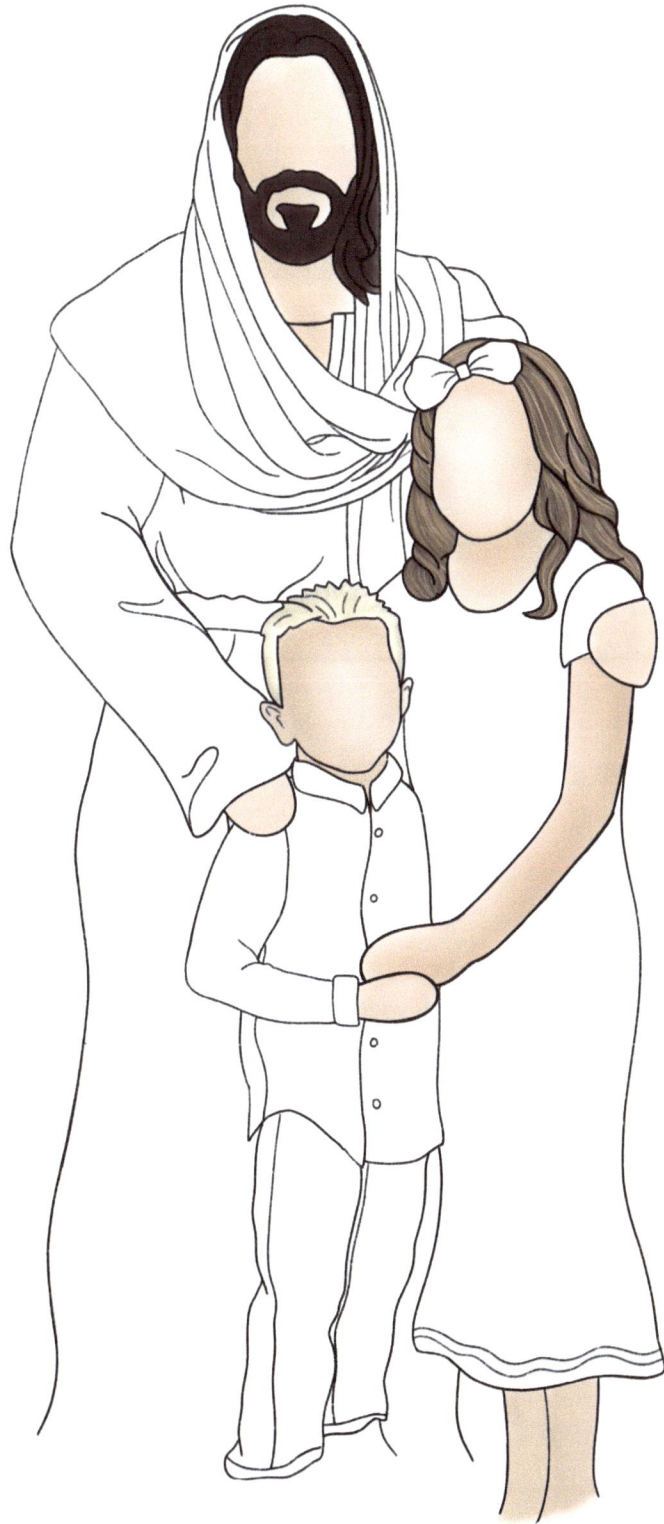

Simplified Glossary

Atonement: Jesus Christ, as the Only Begotten Son of God and the only sinless person to live on this earth, was the only one capable of making an atonement for mankind. This means he suffered and died to pay for our sins. Because of the atonement of Jesus Christ, we can be forgiven of our sins, comforted in our sorrow and pain, and reunited with our loved ones in heaven.

Burial: when a dead body is placed into a coffin which is then put into a hole in the ground and covered with dirt.

Casket/Coffin: the box or case in which the body of a dead person is placed for burial.

Cemetery: an area set apart for the graves, tombs, or funeral urns of the dead.

Counselor: also sometimes called a therapist, this is a trained professional who gives advice or counsel to people who need help healing mentally or emotionally. A grief counselor works primarily with those who are hurting after the death of a loved one.

Cremate: the process of putting a dead body into a fire and burning it to ashes.

Death: the end of life when a person's body and mind stop working. This means that the spirit has left the body which can no longer breathe, see, move, feel, or think.

Dedicatory Prayer: a special prayer given next to the grave where a body will be buried. Sometimes this prayer is given by a religious leader or a member of the family in order to set apart the grave as the final resting spot of the body.

Eternal Families: a phrase used to describe families that can be together forever, not just while they live on earth, but for eternity after the resurrection.

Eulogy: a brief summary of a person's life read at their funeral. Eulogies usually include a description of the deceased's personality, family relationships and experiences, as well as praise for their accomplishments.

Funeral: a ceremony held on behalf of someone who has died to honor and pay tribute to their life.

Funeral Director: also sometimes called a mortician, this is a person who prepares the dead for burial and directs the funeral arrangements.

Funeral Home/Mortuary: a building where the dead are prepared for burial or cremation, where the body may be viewed, and where funeral services can be held.

Funeral Procession: when those attending a funeral get into their cars and drive to the cemetery in one line, usually following the hearse with the coffin of the dead carried inside.

Grave: a hole made in the earth in which to bury a dead body.

Graveside: a funeral service conducted besides the grave of the person about to be buried. This service often includes speakers, songs, and a dedicatory prayer.

Grief: strong mental and emotional suffering or distress that comes as a result of loss or afflictions. Grief can last for a long period of time.

Headstone/Gravestone/Tombstone: a stone marker set at the head of a grave to show where a person has been buried.

Hearse: a vehicle for conveying a dead person to the place of burial.

Memento: an object or item that serves to remind one of a person or past event.

Memorial: something designed to preserve a memory of a person or event. A memorial service is a ceremony that is held after a body has been cremated or buried and serves the same purpose as a funeral to honor and pay tribute to the dead.

Miscarriage: the death of a fetus (a baby who is not fully developed) in utero before it is able to survive outside of the womb.

Pallbearer: a person who carries or attends to a coffin during a funeral or graveside.

Resurrection: the reuniting of the spirit with the body in an immortal state, no longer subject to disease or death. Jesus Christ was the first person on earth to be resurrected and because of His atonement, all mankind will be resurrected after their deaths at the second coming of Jesus Christ.

Stillbirth/Stillborn: the death of a fully developed child right at, or just prior to birth.

Support Group: a group of people who meet regularly to support each other by discussing problems they all have in common, in this case, the death of a loved one.

Urn: a vase for holding the ashes of the cremated dead.

Vault: an outer burial container (usually made of cement) required by the cemetery to prevent the ground from sinking in above the casket.

Viewing: a less formal ceremony where friends and family may come to honor and see the body of the person who has died before their casket is closed for the funeral and burial services. This is also the time when many people come to offer condolences to the closest family members and loved ones of the dead.

Emily Ann Adams holds a degree in English Education and is the creator of Moms of Missing Multiples, a bereavement support group for mothers who are members of the Church of Jesus Christ of Latter-Day Saints who have lost one or more of their multiples. An advocate for exploring the world and embracing diversity, Emily has worked in Mexico teaching English, volunteered with a nonprofit in India to help those afflicted with leprosy and also lived and studied in Paris, France. She and her husband currently live in Southern Utah and are the parents of four living children and one angel son. She is the author of "Is There No Other Way? Exploring Growth Through Grief" and "Loss for Littles: A Guide for Christian Families Dealing with Death".

Ester Ballam Biggs was born and raised in northern Utah where she currently lives with her family of six, their pet cockatiel, hermit crabs, homing pigeons and 8 chickens. Ester holds a Bachelor's of Science in Nursing and currently works as a Registered Nurse helping women in an OBGYN clinic. As much as she loves serving others in the medical field, her greatest joy is being a mother. A champion for the importance of motherhood, Ester currently serves on the board of the Cache Valley Chapter of the Utah Mother's Association. Illustration and calligraphy have always brought Ester joy and respite, and in 2019 she started an online faceless watercolor portrait and calligraphy business, "Small & Simple by Ester." "Loss for Littles: A Guide for Christian Families Dealing with Death" is her debut into illustrating children's books.